Literacy World Satellites

Satellites

Reading and Language Skills Book

When you see this symbol it means you will need a copy of the book.

Heinemann

Contents

* Children will need to read the whole book before doing these activities.

The Lady at the Desk 'Dunnit'

Look at the pictures below.
They show it was the lady at the desk who stole the egg.
Choose a sentence from the box to go with each picture.

1 ______________________

2 ______________________

3 ______________________

4 ______________________

5 ______________________

6 ______________________

She is eating a chocolate bar.

She turns the lights off.

She is reading about the egg in the newspaper.

The bag is hidden in her filing cabinet.

She has long nails.

A chocolate bar wrapper is found near the dinosaur egg case.

Who Said What?

Write out the sentences below adding the correct speakers.

Tom

Mollie

Lady at the desk

Head of Security

Mayor

TV man

1 "Have you come to see the dinosaurs?" said . . .

2 "I'll keep an eye on him," said . . .

3 "My bag has gone!" said . . .

4 "Ow! Someone scratched me!" said . . .

5 "They could put the egg in the bag," said . . .

6 "Sorry, my camera doesn't work in the dark," said . . .

Speech Bubbles

Write the character names and put the words they say into speech bubbles.

e.g. "I want to see T. Rex," said Mollie.

Mollie — *I want to see T. Rex.*

1 "I really like museums," said the strange man.

2 "Stand back for the Mayor!" said the Head of Security.

3 "The case is protected by laser beams," said the Mayor.

4 "The lights have gone out!" said Mollie.

4 "Someone must have taken it!" said Tom.

5 "I know who did it!" said Mollie.

Verbs: Present to Past Tense

The lady at the desk ***picks*** *up the phone.*

The verb in this sentence is in the **present tense**, telling us what is happening now.

The lady at the desk ***picked*** *up the phone.*

The verb in this sentence is in the ***past tense***, telling us what happened in the past.

In these sentences the verbs are underlined.
Write out the sentences changing the verbs from the present tense to the past tense.

1 Tom and Mollie <u>look</u> at the dinosaurs.

2 A crowd of people <u>push</u> past Tom and Mollie.

3 The Head of Security <u>follows</u> the strange man.

4 A TV man <u>points</u> his camera at the case.

5 The Mayor <u>starts</u> to speak.

6 The TV camera <u>zooms</u> in.

7 Suddenly the Mayor <u>screams</u>.

8 Everyone <u>stares</u> at Tom and Mollie.

Syllables

Each 'beat' in a word is called a **syllable**.

Some words have one **syllable**. *e.g. day*

Some words have more than one **syllable**.
e.g. to/day, di/no/saur

A ***Sort the words in the box into four lists using these headings:***
1 syllable 2 syllables 3 syllables 4 syllables

museum	exhibition	teeth	lady
strange	obviously	visiting	people
suddenly	little	room	American

B ***Look at pages 26-27 of* Dinosaur Whodunnit?**
Make a list of:

4 one syllable words

3 two syllable words

1 four syllable word.

Spelling Patterns

A ***Look at the words in the box.***
Sort them into lists with the same letter pattern.
e.g. cake, bake

hook	fake	splash	~~cook~~	fright	crash
book	lake	dash	night	deep	seam
shake	sleep	cream	bright	dream	creep

look	**keep**	**beam**	**take**	**light**	**flash**
cook	______	______	______	______	______
______	______	______	______	______	______
______	______	______	______	______	______

B ***Now add two more words to each list.***

What's Changed?

A ***The play* Jack and the Milk Shake *is based on the story* Jack and the Beanstalk *but some things have been changed.***
***Read the sentences about the* play.**
***Complete the sentences about the* story.**

1 The play is called 'Jack and the Milk Shake'.
The story is called …

2 In the play Jack is going to sell the cow but the little old man has other ideas.
In the story Jack sells …

3 In the play the giant is kind and friendly.
In the story the giant is …

4 In the play the giant tells Jack about a boy who stole his gold, his magic harp and his magic hen.
In the story Jack steals …

5 In the play Jack, the Giant, Mum and the Cow set up a business making strawberry milk shakes.
In the story Jack escapes by …

B ***Which do you like the best – the story or the play?***

I like the play/story best because …

Contractions

An **apostrophe** shows where a letter or letters have been left out of a word. *e.g. I will = I'll*
The word with the apostrophe is called a **contraction**.

A ***Write out the lists.***
Join the words to the correct contractions.

I am	I've
I will	I'm
I have	I'll
I had	I'd

B ***Write out the sentences below, replacing the underlined words with the contractions from the box.***

don't	can't	didn't	haven't	won't	isn't

1. I <u>do not</u> want to meet any more giants.
2. My hair <u>is not</u> really brown.
3. We <u>did not</u> win anything.
4. The giant <u>will not</u> be cross with you.
5. We <u>have not</u> got any money.
6. We <u>cannot</u> sell the cow.

Design a Play Programme

Design a play programme for the play
Little Fred Riding Hood.

Remember to include:

- the title of the play
- where the play is being performed
- what time the play starts
- the names of the people playing the parts.

Adding 'ing'

Words which have a **short vowel sound**, like **hop**, double the last letter before adding **-ing**.
e.g. hop = hopping

Words which **end in e** drop the **e** before adding **-ing**.
e.g. come = coming

A *Add -ing to these words.*

sit → *sitting*		take → *taking*	
live		have	
win		like	
shop		run	
get		make	

B *Write out the sentences below putting in the correct -ing verbs.*

set	shake	help

1 Fred was ____________ off to see his Grandma.

2 The wolf thought he was ____________ Fred.

3 Grandma was ____________ with fear.

Who Said What?

Read the speeches below and write the names of the characters who said them.

Fairy Godfather | Cinderfella | Basil | Bill | Princess

1 "Go upstairs and clean my bedroom." (page 33)

2 "Did you lick Basil's shoes clean?" (page 35)

3 "I wish I was going to the football match." (page 37)

4 "You can have two wishes." (page 38)

5 "Who is the new player in the team?" (page 42)

6 "Be quiet, you two. The match is about to begin." (page 42)

7 "But I got it wrong. You can have three wishes." (page 47)

8 "I wish that Bill and Basil were my servants." (page 47)

Mixed Up Sentences

A ***The Fairy Godfather has mixed up his words.***
Write what he meant to say.
Don't forget the capital letters and full stops.

1 your Godfather am Fairy I

2 can wishes two you have

3 them make will I true come

4 ball you now go can to the

5 your kit all vanish magic will

6 wish left got have you one

7 you what wish are for going to

8 pack your go toothbrushes and

B ***Challenge a friend!***
Choose a sentence from the play and mix up the words. Can your friend sort them out?

Synonyms

Synonyms are words which have similar meanings.
e.g. big, large

A ***Sort the words in the box into synonyms using these headings:***

big **little** **kind** **angry**

great	small	friendly	cross
generous	huge	mad	tiny
furious	large	short	helpful

B ***Write the synonyms from the following sentences.***

1 The classroom was neat and tidy.

2 The cruel, mean monster chased the children.

3 The infant slept in the baby seat.

4 First mend the gate and then repair the fence.

Long and Short Vowels

A ***Sort the words in the box into two lists:***

Words with short vowels	**Words with long vowels**
ran	*came*

swim	~~came~~	got	shout	need	leg	bad
tied	lick	brush	like	gave	just	
fine	race	back	five	~~ran~~	train	thin

B ***All these words have long vowels.***
Sort the words into lists putting together those with long vowels that sound the same.

been	~~great~~	rule	face	neat
rope	cold	hide	flute	high

train	**field**	**tied**	**coat**	**cube**
great				

Design a Poster

Jack and Ella want to find good homes for the kittens. Design a poster to advertise the kittens.

Remember to:

- make the heading clear and eye-catching
- describe the kittens
  e.g. *brown, fluffy*
- make the kittens sound appealing
  e.g. *pretty, playful, funny, friendly*
- explain what the kittens will need
  e.g. *food, shelter, love*
- say where the kittens are
  Pet Rescue Centre
- say when the kittens can be seen
  e.g. *mornings only, after 4 pm*
- give a contact telephone number.

Writing Speech

Speech marks are used at the beginning and end of words which are spoken.

e.g. *"I wish we could find Penny a home," said Ella.* ← full stop

speech marks (↑ at the opening "), comma (↑ after home), speech marks (↑ at the closing ")

Change the speech bubble text into sentences with speech marks. Remember to change the full stops to commas.

Ella

I wish we could find Penny a home.

"I wish we could find Penny a home," said Ella.

Gemma

We've come to choose a dog.

Mum

I wonder why that dog barks so much.

Mr Penrose

She seems a lovely dog.

Jack

So maybe you could give Penny a home.

Verbs: Present to Past Tense

*Mr Penrose **likes** Bouncer.*
The verb **likes** is in the **present tense**.

*Mr Penrose **liked** Bouncer.*
The verb **liked** is in the **past tense**.

A ***Make a list of present tense verbs in the box. Then find the matching past tense verbs.***

eat	speak	told	caught
go	ate	went	spoke
tell	~~run~~	saw	~~ran~~
catch	see	have	had

e.g.	***Present tense***	***Past tense***
	run	*ran*

B ***Write out the sentences putting in the missing verbs.***

1 The teacher ______ the children to go into the hall.

2 ______ your dinner, then you can go out to play.

3 The head teacher ______ to the children in assembly.

4 The policeman ______ the bank robber.

Comprehension

Draw the table below and fill in the gaps.
(Make the boxes big enough to write your notes.)

	The Greyhound	Deep Danger	Old Dog
What pets were rescued?			
Where were the pets found?			tied up in a garden
What was wrong?		the kittens were drowning	
How were the pets helped?	Usman took Flash home		

Alphabetical Order

a b c d e f g h i j k l m n o p q r s t u v w x y z

Look at the alphabet. If the friends were listed in **alphabetical order** they would be: Lee, Raj, Sam.

A ***Write these names in alphabetical order.***

Allan	Tom	Zak	Harmeet	Liam
Ben	Mark	Sandeep	Kate	Emma

If the first letters are the same then look at the **second** letter.

e.g. *fish* *flower* *friend*

B ***Write these words in alphabetical order.***

dog	dish	dragon	duck
milk	man	melon	mosque
snail	slide	seal	sheep

Compound Words

Compound words are made by joining two words together.

e.g. to + night = tonight   no + where = nowhere

Write as many compound words as you can using the words in the box.

moon	man	snow	post	ball
one	body	thing	where	
fire	light	to	time	birth
night	any	every	some	
box	house	day	sun	foot

Scores: ***15 = good***
20 = very good
over 25 = excellent

Plurals

Singular means one of something. *e.g. one* ***dog***

Plural means more than one of something. *e.g. two* ***dogs***

A ***Sort the words in the box into two lists using these headings:*** **Singular Plural**

friend	match	lady	baby
babies	bags	box	matches
bag	boxes	friends	ladies

1 Which words made the plural by adding **s**?

2 Which words made the plural by adding **es**?

3 Which words made the plural by changing **y** into **ies**?

B ***Write the plurals of these words.***

girl watch jelly fox car puppy

Fill in the Gaps

A ***Write out the sentences putting in the missing words.***

1. "My dad said he will take us to the ________ tonight," said Raj.
2. "I can't go to the fair because I haven't got any ________," said Lee.
3. "You can ________ my car," said Sam's dad.
4. "I don't have any ________ for you," said Raj's mum.
5. The woman gave Lee ________ pounds.

B ***Write out the lists.***
Join the things that go together.

Sam's dad	Micky
Mrs Green	car
little girl	purse
woman	baby
Lee's mum	ball

Adjectives

Adjectives are describing words. *e.g. little, old*

Nouns are naming words. *e.g. car, house*

Adjectives describe **nouns**. *e.g. little car, old house*

A ***Sort the words in the box into two lists using these headings:* Adjectives Nouns**

delicious shopping dirty
ghost train scary best heavy
car friends candy floss

B ***Write out the sentences putting in the missing adjectives from your list.***

1 Lee, Sam and Raj were __________ friends.

2 The __________ car needs cleaning.

3 The woman was carrying a bag of __________ shopping.

4 The friends bought some __________ candy floss.

5 They had a ride on the __________ ghost train.

Comprehension

A ***Answer the questions in complete sentences.***

1 What news did Raj tell Sam? (page 3)
Raj told Sam …

2 What did Sam want to do at the fair? (page 5)
Sam wanted …

3 Why couldn't Lee go to the fair? (page 7)
Lee couldn't go to the fair because …

4 What was the first job that the friends did? (page 11)
The first job the friends did was …

5 What did Lee do with the purse? (page 31)
Lee gave the purse …

B ***If you had five pounds to spend at the fair, what would you spend it on?***

If I had five pounds to spend I would …

Sequencing

A ***Write out the sentences in the correct order to tell the story. The first one is done for you.***

1 The children were on a school trip.

The coach driver called an ambulance.

The injection saved her life.

Kim rolled into a bee's nest.

The ambulance men gave Kim an injection.

Kim became very ill.

She was allergic to bee stings.

B ***Kim was allergic to bee stings.***
Make a list of five other things people can be allergic to.

Words Within Words

Some words have shorter words within them.
e.g. ***anything*** = *a an any thin I in thing*
anyone = *a an any on one*

A *How many words can you find within these words?*

allergic

frightened

forgot

someone

uninteresting

information

B *Challenge a friend!*

Find a long word in the dictionary. Copy it out carefully.
Find all the shorter words within your word.
Can your friend find as many words as you?

Pronouns

Pronouns are words that stand in for nouns.

e.g. Shane = noun he = pronoun

Other **pronouns** are: I she we they it

Write out the story putting in the missing pronouns.

Shane went to stay on a farm. ________ liked to help the farmer. Gran and Grandad said Shane followed the farmer everywhere.

"You are like a shadow," ________ said.

"Can ________ help you?" Shane asked Mr Jones.

"Yes," said Mr Jones. "________ will get the tractor. ________ is in the barn. Then ________ can plough the field together."

Word Ladders

You can make a word ladder by changing one letter on each rung. Each change must make a new word.

e.g.

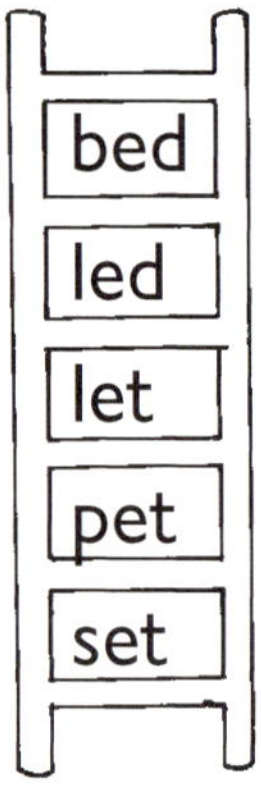

ran

run

big

hear

feed

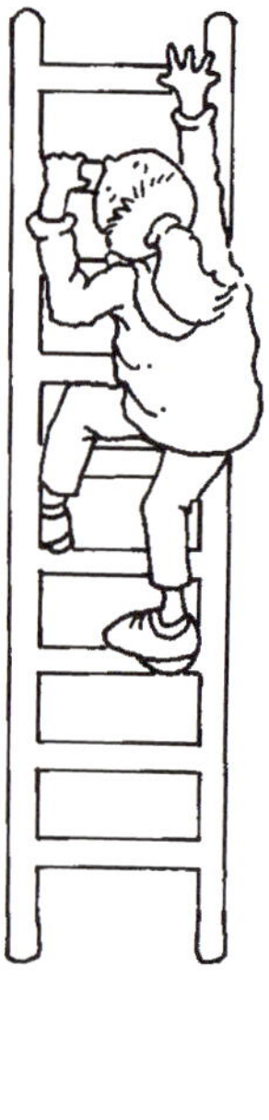

How Did They Feel?

A **_Complete the sentences choosing words from the box._**

surprised	worried	happy	relieved
lucky	concerned	bored	terrified
scared	safe	frightened	anxious

1 After it had rained all day Holly and Josh felt ________ .

2 When Josh saw the river was high he felt ________ .

3 When the engine went dead Dad felt ________ .

4 When Josh said "We're all going to drown." He felt ________ .

5 When Holly heard the helicopter she felt ________ .

6 When they were rescued they all felt ________ .

B **_How would you feel if you were trapped in a flood? Write three sentences to describe your feelings._**

If I was trapped in a flood I …

Capital Letters and Full Stops

A sentence begins with a **capital letter** and ends with a **full stop**.
People's names begin with **capital letters**.
e.g. ***S**o **H**olly and **J**osh ran to the car and climbed in**.***

A ***Rewrite the passage putting in the capital letters and full stops.***

the river was very high dad's car drove into the dip the dip was full of water the engine cut out holly josh and dad were trapped dad used his mobile phone a rescue helicopter came to rescue them they were lucky to be alive

B ***Rewrite the passage putting in the capital letters and moving the full stops to the correct places.***

dad slammed on the. brakes then the car. swung round dad. pulled on the steering wheel the. car slid from side to. side and stopped